The Wind Told Me So

A Collection Of Poems

S.J. Poetry

THE WIND TOLD ME SO

CONTENTS

I began writing this collection of poems on the premise that I could recall impressions, moments, and reactions that I felt after meeting and establishing trust between special someones. I dedicate this book to you all.

I also dedicate this book to the few people who helped me on this, you are an inspiration, and I am grateful to know who you are. -S.J.

FORCEFIELD

A forcefield
shielded me
from self-doubt
I'm still amazed
by its strength.

WRITTEN

You
should never ever judge
a book by its width

Because if you do

you might
misinterpret something
well written
or even
miscalculate
what you read
while measuring
the length of a page

Born and raised in the South
I know there was an emancipation
of slaves
Even after slavery
sin tensed
and they would run on for days
The bright children
stood upright
praising a Sunday
worth recording

My Great-Granny
half-white posing in one of my

favorite photos

My Great-Great Granddaddy
must've been
an Irish immigrant
because Ancestry DNA tells me
I'm 10 percent caucasian
and 4 percent is Irish blood

I miss someone I've never met,
It's strange

It's days I feel blessed
when I think of the wars
occurred in Africa

My skin was never
a drum to beat on,
Music enlightens me like sun,
and I feel grateful
to breathe clean air and drink
fresh water

I ponder on how to be still like a pond
So still,
I astral plane
and see myself ultra-violet
Brilliant enough to begin a new idea
or bloom a movement of energy
wavering for me
to define its presence
with skillful purpose

Its passion hiding underneath

words spoken
People notice when you speak,
but never ever judge a book by its width

nor hold your tongue
if it will make a sad person smile

Why is because
that might just be the fraction
that makes you whole
or
the index to new ideas.

TO SPEAK OR NOT TO SPEAK

Speak what needs to be heard
More importantly
listen to what is said
to know thoughts brought to light

In solitude know thyself
although
new thoughts create
know what is true to your well being

love continues
to thrive
in a healthy conscience
because of discernment.

LET ME TELL YOU ABOUT THE PARTY

Let me tell you about the party

greet the floor with dance

across the hall
I see two lovers hold hands
A man whispers to a young woman
"I love you."
standing in a doorway

music plays
threads flutter
like butterflies under moonlight

young men fanning
like fire hydrants
loose in summertime

people soaked in their own heat.

THE WIND TOLD ME SO

Because the wind told me so
I prayed for you
a thousand times
until trees shook their spines
We are growing closer
I think it's because of the
stories we share
I've come to think of
stories as leaves
When I listen
with my good ear
there's a sort
of photosynthesis

You are always
liberated
in the fancy photos
you brag to me
I too am a breeze
A captured song
bestowed beneath stars

We should make
memories of play
like the first time
soft mud touches clean hands
We will wash ours
and then have dinner

Your impression means to me
what a fork
means to a mouth
In my newsfeed I scroll for you
excessively
like a constitution
made to keep me civil
when I feel more than
wild to wonder
too wise to not know
what those clock eyes
are watching

Our time
is valuable
like
intelligent answers
Life's tests
seem to present themselves
whenever
you are not around
It's historic
the way your voice
reminds my bones
they have sensory
Although
having never been plagued,
I have felt complete blackness
at a moment
your light could have existed
as the beacon
I desperately needed

whenever we meet

*I know warmth
like two hands pressed together*

*Please know
I prayed for you.*

INTUITION

For a very long time

it has been "sound"

caressing the ear canals

Felt by intuitive listeners

Felt like hands
of cave carvers
coding history

imprinting signs in formation of Earth
that still wave
in our present

they were suggesting to think
before one decides to speak

The wind hums
and reminds me of a child
with fingers crossed behind its back

The ocean roars

praising the Earth's crust
for clinging to its core
very correctly

and I imagine so loud
my thoughts become words.

BOUQET

There is a place
where all men can
decide who they love
forever

Today I am
a product of
the curve of your lips
An imprint of desire
An ash from the star
in your eye

I've climbed expectations
and standards of men
just to feel you freedom
like speech

Abroad the continent of
your thought process
I am but a traveler
I've packed surprises
in hopes you're tired of
old baggage

I've cleaned myself up
so many times
I feel like a cloud

that never tarnishes
my judgement

I see your hips
as if
I'm just a droplet
in a rainbow
A man on the other side
of the seed
that will become
your bouquet of flowers.

(UNTITLED)

A great wisdom
brings clarity
In times of doubtfulness
It breathes
like a wind from on high
grazing the surface of a dream
to awaken the inner man
once again
after a long
slumber inside oneself.

NATURAL WOMAN

Your love is the surface
I want to explore
A massage
could be therapy

time has prescribed my hands for you

I have thought clouds
I accumulate cumulus ideas
and think of cunninglingus

There's a world out there but
I have plans
to voyage you my love

A voyeur would simply dream of you

I desire deltas of you atop bedsheets

Hike me
your claws won't
hurt this sovereign soul
I know nature
and woman there are flowers in the wind
when you speak
Your eyes
sum up the sunset
when you blink

The new day are your kisses
I am speechless as a cave
in wilderness

My bedroom
was a glacier
before your eyes
warmed me inside its interior design
I have climbed pyramids of light
for you
my atlas of ecstasy.

I LOVE ME SOME ME

I know who I am

An embodied soul
in communication
with my morality
yet still becoming

I love who I am
although
I want to be more sensible
knowing sympathy more
Sympathy is like
a flickering flame
aloft in winter's cold
the flame is
unbothered to man's eye

against the
harsh winter wind of humaness
something causes it to curl
and dance
tribal-like in a war
the war the eye does not see
like the soul of a man.

ART FORM

I am
no stranger to creative thinking
The imagination I have
is determined
It's never been
friends with failure
My creativity is near to me
Success is my friend
an art form
I've grown fond of.

THE DAWN OF A NEW AGE

The dawn
of a new age

is only the distance
of one moment away

At any second

we can become
who we are to be
and know what is to learn

maneuvering the crevice
of intellect
to discover light lit
in a once dark place

There are lessons learned from practice

The present
is a preparation of continuity
for next generations
The future
is a flurry of fascination
whizzing in vibrations

people

places
things

facts torn from fiction

pages written in faith
made into substance

Healing for lost hopes

Proof of past times
to improve those
in search of a better way

We will and they will
continue because of goodness

Mercy will cycle like always
Just as the new sun
and clouds and rain

The trees will breed
and we will breathe well
Laughter
on top of bright conversations
sparking innovation
to carry God's very own
conscious bodies

With grace
the planet will spin
and circumstances will change

But the stars will never be forgotten

they will shine
and our minds will echo the wisdom.

FREE FROM ANXIETY

"Never worry about tomorrow"
they say

"Tomorrow," calls its
friend "Today"

"Tomorrow" calls
"Today" and says,
"Don't worry, we'll figure everything out when you
get here."

Stress is not medicine
Don't take that shit

I know prayer is a remedy

Tomorrow
is religion
for believers and well-doers
Believe in it

Anxiety is a curse you can break if
you bow to freedom
Practice churning the wind inside your lungs
Know that breathing is a blessing
"Never worry"
I say.

TRUTH

I know very well
life is worth the activity
Since ancient
precious gifts have kindled
from fires deep within
I know
waiting to see faith
inner-work into truth
is worth goodness.

FOR THE CAUSE

"I'm the guy
that roll down his car window
and flick a booger
while it's raining.

It's not litter
I don't want to
ruin my interior."

That was a joke

You see
it's hard to push buttons
if someone makes
you feel inferior

I'm no menace to society
I'm a mirror to my mental

Keep your distance
if I feel offended

It's a limit
but I might be into you

Used to hide the liquor
in the dresser drawer

I still insist on pretty women
All my friendships feel like swimming pools
cause' I be in the clear
and people try to flex the rules

We went from
jungle gym to jungle juice
to Gin-n-Juice
and gentrification

The ginseng was warm with honeydew

and the pen was my favorite tool too

Now I prefer my cellular
It's different women calling me
and they prefer the finest furs
It's been my destiny for God
to use me with the words

The whip too clean
I watch the curb

I never purge
only observe.

TIME

*My senses
have never surrendered
to false presence*

You exist to me

There are words we share

*and we touch like
hot cocoa hands
under snowflake blankets
melting*

*Is it you or me
or the seasons changing for us?*

You echo on these walls

*I'm left speechless
as a man
who found water after a drought of rain,
drinking.*

You quench my thirst most days

*I have love for you
my love*

I hold you
like a tune
in this city full of songwriters

When we're together
I have a refreshing vibe of excellence
It might be God
writing love notes for us to dance too.

WE HAPPEN

*It's not the way you
doubt me
that makes me
want to prove
myself*

*It's the way you look at me
with hoping eyes
full of blackness*

*It's never
how you ignore
my efforts
causing me
to spill into
your free time flawlessly
but
it's the reminiscence
of your touch
against my skin
longing for your brightest
ideas of partnership*

*We use kind words
because they communicate better
It's never the shallowness
of lust that
breeds my desire*

*but your voice and when it
reverberates against surfaces
I am responsive
with depth of emotion.*

ACTUALIZING

There's a soul and a body
to me
I not only exercise my mind
I exercise my sovereignty

All I am
is a chain
of God's grace

All I am
is a structure
of significant worth.

FOREVER AND A DAY

Today
live freely
in the eyes of you
Walk on the bridge
that doesn't burn
into tomorrow
jocosely
Promises kept
will hug you back that way
So mean what you say
with your own words
knowing exactly where
they came from.

ORNAMENT

When you grab a wish
it's actually ornament
because it too
holds onto something

We know that miracles
happen daily
Think of what can
instead of that opposite

The cold
is a refreshing feel
for those who
have been in
some hot shit
so be courteous
to those
misinformed
of adversity

We are able
of having a blessing
if blesser allows

and too much of
anything
is bad for you
they say

that's why
you should watch
what you wish for.

I WILL NEVER FEAR LIFE

What is it you wish to know
again?

Speak dreams reborn for me
please

The atmosphere is brighter that way

Shake off fear like the last time
you defeated doubt
that kept you from planning greatness

Fly somewhere awesome into
brilliance begging for a repeat

Say to yourself
"The only enemy I have is myself"

I know all of my secrets

I win
I win some more

for me
for tomorrow

The future all started

and I stood.

DAYDREAMING

I know
I'm a dreamer

Because the clouds feel like
salt baths on my tongue sometimes
when it rains
I feel like I got washed gold in
my pocket

Like I been sifting through a
sandstorm
or building a metal detector for my mind

You know the difference between a hope
and a doubt
is only perception to what your eyes
can calculate

I have the fondest memory
of my most precious...
my most precious dream

and it was daytime with
the entire world on
display

only I saw what I wanted
because I am a dreamer.

GIVING GIFTS

I bought a gift
knowing gifts are worth
something more than nothing

So I hope you like it
at least

I used to think
of myself as an
entrepreneur of emotion

I could patent a smile
so no one could claim
that which they did not
create themselves

I hope you love who you are

I hope your soul never sells

You don't have permission
Who told you,
you could due that?

And I know this is hard to understand
but I already forgave you
for everything in this world
that didn't make me happy

*I'm not perfect
but I got you this gift anyway
I hope you like it.*

I STILL WAIT

*I race
my mind
when I see you*

*back to the times of
affection
in the nature of love
we were wild
there when I think back*

*the promises kept
are why we made it this far*

*It's something about that
question you begged*

*I'm giving you
what you want today*

*And we can make time
again for an exchange of us*

I like my space too

*I more than like you
we grow on each other*

It's affection

And when I think about it...
it's been a long time
you and I
doing this thing.

WANDERLUST

*I am settling into the best
of your exuberance*

*I am but a prayer waiting to hatch
into your most precious*

A cup of forever and a day

Ultra smart and beautiful

*Let me kiss you the way secrets
release loyalty*

*Slow and strong,
soft and golden,
compassion-filled-joyous-moments
of wanderlust unabashed.*

OLD TALE

A conquerer
though not arrogant

the way young men
who became kings to young
fell

He held excellency up
by the armored parts
and brushed off the cobwebs
that hung raggedly, cold,
and withered

The weathering exceptions
and prices
of too good
to be trues
were uncompelling
to what
he saw praiseworthy

He chose to treasure
his devoutness
the way gold lies buried
beneath sands of ancient
wars of all the
renamed kingdoms

Reprised possession
of a soul was his own

decorated key carved delicately
how he handles the first
word told

A memory from the wisest of
forests and campfires
warming creation.

FREE

For you

only a portion

For me

only
what I need
and all of what I want
is clear
but
the necessity is stored

For you

all you thought
would come to pass
is decided for
destiny

For me

it is written well
and on time
the course
is made

No sadness for me

only tranquil

only
designed fortresses and
pleasant aromas

new scent complete
filled atmospheric passions
perfected

For you

is up to you

For me

to be thankful always
and cherish it.

IT WON'T BE A PAPER SACK

I saw you
a tremble in the
pouring rain
like a glass tinkered by a
silver spoon
damp ringing clean
off your leather coat

The sun dripped
over the other clouds

You were hoping for a light
I saw you
half the distance from happiness
but one step closer to me
I was two steps
from your direction
We were brought together
simply because this is down south

It must have been magnetism
or mannerisms
I don't know exactly
but our souls caught
up
You know solar panels are
gaining popularity

I really like your hat
You bring to mind a cleaner world
calendars from this filth
We should watch the solar system

Lines are being made
We should grab lunch
no paper sacks

they'll get wet
and fall apart.

OBSERVATORY

If you fall
I'm there to catch you

Then I bow
like a tilted telescope
after capturing
a comet

Just for fun I pick up a
ton of red paper hearts
and blow them at you

You laugh
I show you the room
It's no danger
baby
lay on my chest
adrift in the sea
which is my compassion
I watch you sleep
stokedly
like a yell
in the desert

you're thinking about
something vast
I think about how
to quarantine you from a sick

and selfish world
while regretting the quicksand
that is the sweat of my palms
because you cause nervousness
must be the river
that is your hair

sometimes
I feel like all the stars in
the night sky
are a reflection of you

I think you admire me
but I'm just an observatory
You make
men awe
all scientifically

Women
are THE most interesting
creation on this planet
that's why I'm there to catch you
like pricelessness or infinite value.

SURE

*I yearn for a powerful
sureness
Powerful like the
time that never waits
Preferred
like the fruit that grows
from trees
Stemming in my
own confidence
It's the adjuration for
insight
It's reach for a new day
to do great
and live
for the man
I've always
wanted to be.*

ALL THAT SAVING

The wind blows

It's been hot as hell in here

Someone explain to me
why I feel freedom
wash over
like every ancestor of mine
sent me a letter
in the same
envelope

my pride
opens the reward
with prize joy

like I got a taste of
resolution after an
internalized war

felt like forever
in there.

I NEED MY ANGELS

I dream of you
in this life
like you never wandered away
Never swam the mysteries of last breaths
into new creation
This universe still has you I know
This planet still knows your footprints
It knows your DNA
Never leave me
this way
I hope your okay
I hope you're different
so your light can impress the creator
all luminescent

When you speak to him
tell him about us
tell him about life
without fear
I dream of you

May my mind find peace
and may my angels stay near
God knows how much I need you here.

WATER IN MY CUP

In life
you can see the cup as half empty
or half full
or drink the water with your hands.

UNTOUCHED

I'm no storm drain
willing to collect the excess
spit of talk
you've spewed to men
who were serious
about their
own words

I am a tower made
from the finest
collection
of God material

A wishing well for a soul
with my own pocket change
No strange or stranger has
ever harmed
what I've protected as
truth untouched
I know there are corners
You can't walk over me
hoping the alley of lies
you love will lead to a heaven
somewhere.

THE WORTHY THINGS YOU DO

I still need you
like a dream needs
eyes

I've been awake all night

you remind me of the moon
but you're not here

I wish you were close
the way tic is to toc

or the way wind calms the rain

I'm more natural near you

Your voice is like the space
where I find
my favorite memorabilia

when you pray
your hands
interweave
like tied up work boots

I want you to know,

there's a blessing in the
worthy things you do

I know you're working on you,
I'm working on me too

An orderly fashion of a soul
A manuscript of praise
for a spirit

Two instruments for feet
walking in the voice of God

Faith
is enlightenment from the
creator himself
We will serve him
How does that sound
the next time we meet?
A soul with
a soulmate
oh lovely it shall surely be.

I HAD A QUESTION

First
they tell you
they love you
then the people change

The leaves change colors

The raindrops sound
different in late autumn
because the branches
turn into drumsticks

The coins in my pocket
got dew on em'
I miss the magic in summertime
The sun rhymes with frying pan
"It's no way I'm going out there man!"
loud and clear

Orange citrus remedy for me
No make that ice cube tray
so I don't fall off a sidewalk
Remember when they started
putting bacon on everything?

The times are different now
but I got a dollar
all folded up

in the side of my wallet
like a crush note
But don't worry
this love letter won't reach you
in time
because I got
to find a stamp
before the weather turns bad.

THIS LOVE LETTER

Mam
You really have the
urge to convey your
neediness of my love
at this moment?
I already gave you what
I had in store
I'm in overdrive
crafting new
emotions to feed your desire
for wholeness
This is how it feels
catering to you
honey please be grateful
I'm only
a man
who must love
himself first.

(UNTITLED)

Every other day
I feel responsible for
the awesomeness
of men like me

It's a group thing
like birds that flock
we fly different
and I get higher
to becoming my best self.

GET WITH IT

In life
important steps are made
On occasion
I skip
hop
jump
over obstacles
just to reach euphoria
When I plan
my vision is narrow as a horses head
sometimes
and I tread
like pollen on
butterfly wings
The flowers get jealous
because of synchronicity
I plant wisdom on a bed of dreams
wishing for brighter tomorrows
that run wild and free.